STEAM MEMOR   's

No. 39: LOCOMOTIVES AWAITING DISPOSAL

Locations include the Eastern, Midland, Southern, Western, North East and Scottish Regions

Copyright Book Law Publications 2009
ISBN 978-1-907094-43-9

INTRODUCTION

Even when they were cold, laid-up, redundant or at the very doors of eradication, the steam locomotive still had something which drew our attention. Luckily, many railway photographers felt the same way and so we have on record many thousands of images of steam locomotives waiting to make the final journey to the scrap yard or already resident within one. Those images show numerous aspects of the 'dead' steam locomotive; solo shots, group shots, looking up, looking down, looking along seemingly endless lines. All are poignant, some dramatic, whilst others are simply a record.

Except for one example, everything within these pages was either cut up, broken up, or dismantled, and then finally obliterated in some furnace at home or abroad. This lot are pure history, memories which one day will fade from those who knew them and managed to record the final moments.

Besides the photographic contributions from Keith Pirt and Don Beecroft, we have included some from Malcolm Castledine, who managed to take a few choice 'views' of locomotives in precarious situations waiting for the chop. George Devine is another contributor who made a point of visiting the scrap yards and scrap lines in order the capture on film the final images of a steam locomotive waiting for the call to oblivion.

Dedicated to Mike Lake - a true Gentleman who would have appreciated the images herein.

(*Title page*) **The waiting for these three 'Clans' is almost over. Having been stored for some considerable time at Polmadie engine shed, they were hauled to Darlington in September 1963 so that North Road scrapyard could do the necessary. The trio are seen on the works lines at Bank Top engine shed and consist No.72000, 72003 and 72001. All are minus coupling and connecting rods but have managed to keep the sacks over their chimneys. On arrival, these Pacifics, along with sisters 72002 and 72004, caused considerable interest amongst the trainspotting community and many an unplanned trip was made to Darlington to see them but you had to be quick because they were soon dealt with by the ever efficient lads with the gas torches. Although not properly discernible from this angle, the tender attached to No.72003 was still wearing the pre-1957 BR emblem.** *David Dunn collection.*

Printed and bound by
The Amadeus Press, Cleckheaton, West Yorkshire

First published in the United Kingdom by
Book Law Publications, 382 Carlton Hill, Nottingham, NG4 1JA

Shortly after Nationalisation the Western Region made a concerted effort to get rid of the locomotives which the Great Western had inherited from the South Wales companies it had absorbed in previous times. On 11th October 1953 these four examples of 0-6-2 tank engines, of which only Nos.434 and 155 are identifiable, stood outside Swindon works waiting their turn to be broken up. The former Brecon & Merthyr 0-6-2T, No.434, which was ex Cardiff Cathays shed, had just been withdrawn but it was apparently not scrapped until the following September - Swindon had a habit of using these locomotives on internal duties within the works, basically getting every bit of usefulness out of them before dismantling them. It was later seen on Swindon works dump on 22nd August 1954, still intact. Next in line was ex Cardiff Railway 4F 0-6-2T No.155, which was the last of three such engines built for the erstwhile CR in 1908 by Kitson & Co. The other two had been condemned during the Grouping leaving this sole survivor working from Cardiff East Dock shed. Unlike the B&M 0-6-2T, No.155 was cut up shortly after this scene was captured on film. The third engine in line looks like a Taff Vale 'A' class with the original round topped side tanks but its number has eluded the writer. *BLP - KRP 101.*

Another six-coupled tank from South Wales recently arrived at Swindon for cutting up on 11th October 1953 was ex Rhymney Railway 'S' class 4F 0-6-0T No.95, from Cardiff East Dock shed. Formerly GWR No.610, it was the first of its four-strong class to be condemned, the others, also allocated to 88B Cardiff East Dock, all followed No.95 to the scrap yard in early 1954. When built in 1908 by Hudswell, Clarke & Co., they were supplied with round-top boilers but from 1930 onwards the Great Western started to put their mark on them by fitting taper boilers with the Belpaire type firebox as seen here. Their first GWR numbers were 608, 609 and 611. In the 1946 renumbering scheme they were allocated Nos.93, 94 and 96 but only the latter engine took the number up. The RR had three other similar 4F 0-6-0T (Nos.604, 605, 606, latterly 90, 91, 92) which the company acquired from Hudswell, Clarke in 1920 and which were classified 'S1'. They too were got rid of in 1954 but they had kept their original Belpaire boilers to the end so the GWR/BR(WR) certainly got their moneys' worth from them, even though they only worked for thirty-four years. *BLP - KRP 103.*

In 1919 the Alexandra Docks Co. purchased a pair of 0-6-0 tank engines from the Ministry of Munitions. Barely two years old, the outside cylinder engines had been built by Kerr Stuart & Co. in August 1917 and were an in-house design supplied to the Railway Operating Division 'off the shelf'. As can be seen, they were robust looking engines and weighing in at 50 tons apiece were ideal for the purpose of shunting heavy trains through less than ideal trackwork. This is No.667 of the pair, and is heading the breakdown train at Newport Pill (86B) engine shed on a rather and damp 12th June 1954. Whatever its duties entailed at this time, they were certainly less than arduous because the veteran was ready for retirement and by November would be resident at Swindon works ready for breaking up. Its twin, No.666, also shedded at 86B lasted until the following April but the inevitable caught up with that 0-6-0T too. *BLP - KRP 4F.8.1.*

Eight months after withdrawal from Ebbw Junction shed, former Brecon & Merthyr 0-6-2T No.435 still carries the 86A shedplate on the smokebox door. The date is 22nd August 1954 and the location is Swindon Locomotive Works. No.435 is, or was up to this particular weekend, still active as one of the works shunters but now apparently its time is up and some mechanical problem has overcome its precarious existence. Also still in situ at this late date is the front numberplate but the brass cabsides have long gone (were they melted down or did either of them survive into private ownership - the editor would like to know please), replaced by a crudely painted or is that chalked identification instead. In the right background can seen one of the Robinson ROD 2-8-0s, No.3024, acquired by the Great Western many years previously. The ex Canton engine was in shops for a minor overhaul before returning to traffic at a new home shed at Pontypool Road. *BLP - KRP 19H.8.6.*

Swindon scrap yard in all its glory or should that be 'In all its inglorious majesty'? In reality this was once the concentration yard where locomotives gathered before being sent off to the cutting-up shop, however, the scrapping business became so busy that this yard itself took on the role as scrap yard. The date is 23rd June 1963 and a number of engines are waiting to be dealt with. We have no individual numbers to fall back on but the types and classes can be made out with care. On the left we have a Mogul, then the yard's mobile crane. Heading the main throng is a de-tanked Prairie followed by a 94XX, two 'Halls', another Prairie, a 'Castle', an 0-6-0PT, with three more 'Halls' bringing up the rear. The sole 'Castle' was apparently No.5023, one of 82C's own allocation which had been withdrawn during the previous February. The nearest 'Prairie' was No.6119 with 6101 being identified as the intact example. Our five 'Halls' comprised Nos.5912, 5931, 5945, 5993 and 5995, which had originated from the likes of Banbury, Old Oak Common, Oxford, Reading and Oxley, in that order although some of them had been resident in the works premises since earlier in the year. This vista of the scrapyard does not encompass the whole area, indeed to the left and right were further lines of engines waiting their turn for the chop or, in some cases, sale to private scrapyards. *Malcolm Castledine.*

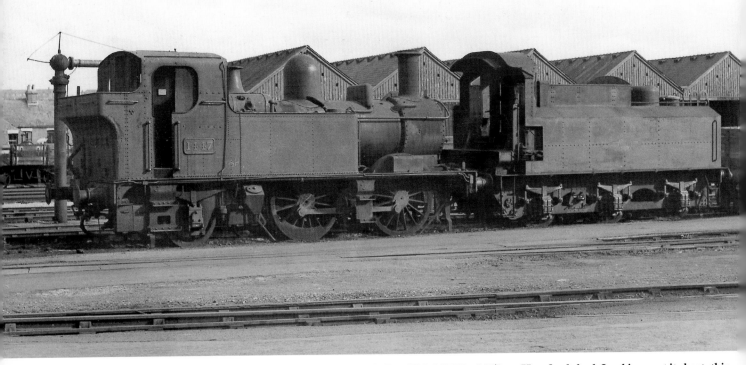

A recent arrival at Swindon for examination on 9th April 1964 was Collett 1P 0-4-2T No.1447, ex Hereford shed. Looking past its best, this engine had certainly been around the system since Nationalisation and had worked at Reading, Oxford, Oswestry, Slough, Radyr, Croes Newydd and Hereford in that order. But the day of reckoning had arrived and it would not leave Swindon again but, between this date and eventual breaking up in July, the little tank engine put in a bit of shunting at the works. Note the tender buffered up to the 0-4-2T is one of the LMS Ivatt 3500 gallon types normally coupled to the 4F 2-6-0s. This example has a recess for the tablet exchange apparatus so was probably once attached to one of the M&GN allocated engines. Now about this time Swindon was repairing engines from other regions, especially the Eastern and Midland regions (known during the Fifties' as Inter Regional Assistance) and amongst the classes being dealt with were Ivatt 4F 2-6-0s. In April 1964 half a dozen of the class were evident at Swindon so that tender must be from one of those 'visitors'. *Malcolm Castledine.*

Shortly before the mass intake of withdrawn British Railways steam locomotives at Barry, the Western Region had sold a number of condemned locomotives to Woodham Bros. whose storage yard was at Barry works. On 24th September 1966 the place had just a few lines of engines stored and waiting to be taken into the cutting-up area. Amongst the batch of 43XX class 4MT 2-6-0s present was this scruffy No.5322 which totally intact except for the usual items, number plates and shed plate. Withdrawn in April 1964, this engine was one of the last of the 53XX batch and had certainly given the GWR and WR a good account of itself since being put into traffic in August 1917. Latterly it had been shedded at Pontypool Road and was stored there after withdrawal until Woodham's bought it in 1965. Prior to being allocated to 86G, it was variously at Swindon, Tyseley, Reading, Oxford and Didcot. In 1969 it was to return to that latter place after being rescued from Barry scrap yard, one of the first of dozens of engines which were to be successfully preserved after years of neglect. No.5322 became part of the Great Western Society collection at the former BR motive power depot site - the rest is history. To date the engine has not quite spent an equal amount of time preserved as it did in traffic for its former owners but its probably a safe bet to say it will surpass its previous lifespan. *Malcolm Castledine.*

(*opposite*) When the Western Region withdrew the first of the 'Kings' in February 1962, Wolverhampton Stafford Road based No.6006 KING GEORGE I, the trainspotting world drew a breath in astonishment and realised that if the 'Kings' were not safe then nothing was. Reality had hit home and within four months seven more had been condemned. As if to ram the point home, the Western Region got rid of the whole class by the end of the year. At Stafford Road shed where fifteen of the class resided before withdrawal, many of them languished in the open through the severe winter of 62/63 waiting for the call to Swindon or the visit of the scrap merchants' representative. No.6022 was one of those 84A engines which stuck out the winter in the shed yard and in this 24th February 1963 illustration the elements are still clinging to the engine and its companion 'King' with a vengeance. Note that the name, number and shed plates have long been removed since its withdrawal in September. There was nothing wrong with No.6022 at the time it was withdrawn and its condemnation was simply a result of taking the engine out of service at the end of the summer timetable with a view that it would never return to traffic again. Surprisingly, in view of all the diesel failures which occurred during the following winter, these 4-6-0s were never reinstated to work like many other 'stored' engines during that period. The other dead 'Kings' present at Stafford Road on this February day were: Nos.6007, 6012, 6014, 6015 and 6017, whilst Nos.6001 and 6002 had recently departed for Cox & Danks Ltd. at Oldbury. The other five would join them over the ensuing months. *Malcolm Castledine.*

Nos.6017 and 6014 certainly appear to be somewhat unwanted too. *Malcolm Castledine.*

MIDLAND REGION

On a visit to Barrow engine shed on Sunday 28th August 1955, Keith Pirt found this former Furness Railway 0-6-0 heading a long line of stored engines, many of which would never work again. No.52494 was one of five surviving Pettigrew designed 3Fs from a class which once numbered nineteen engines. The five were also the only Furness engines still extant in 1955. Amongst the survivors, this engine was unique in having the only Furness round-top boiler which it acquired from withdrawn No.52508 in 1951. The others all had Belpaire boilers, like No.52501 behind, fitted by the LMS at Horwich. Built in 1913 by North British Locomotive Co., as FR No.1, No.52494 was also the oldest of the survivors but not for much longer because this particular period of storage would take it through the winter and into 1956 when it was condemned in May. Before Grouping, this class, known as 'Red Indians' by those who worked and knew them (perhaps the Indian red livery had some bearing), were the elite amongst the FR goods engines and were equally happy hauling heavy slow mineral trains or fast merchandise van trains. Latterly this 0-6-0 was allocated to Moor Row but when that shed closed in 1954 it went to Workington and still wears the 12D shed plate on its smokebox door, however, during October it was officially transferred to Barrow. Although not sacked, which was usual elsewhere, the chimney has a flat plate, with a heavy object to weight it down, covering the orifice. No.52501 was also transferred to Barrow in October 1955 but survived the winter storage. In December 1956 it moved to Carnforth and worked until condemned in July 1957 as the penultimate member of the 'Red Indians' class. Although both Workington and Moor Row were in the Carlisle Upperby motive power area 12, as 12D and 12E respectively, it is of interest to know that they sent their engines for storage to 11B Barrow which was in the Carnforth motive power area - old habits die hard - but Barrow depot did have a surplus of siding space, especially in BR days. Modellers note the bufferstop which is bereft of any cross bars - now that's different. *BLP - KRP 97F.5.*

When this picture of ex Midland 2P 4-4-0 No.40536 was captured at Barrow in August 1955, the engine had just celebrated its fifty-sixth birthday and was destined to work until it was just three months shy of its sixtieth anniversary. However, during the period before Grouping, the Johnson designed engine had been rebuilt twice, firstly by Deeley and later by Fowler. It was during the latter rebuild that new frames were included which, added to the new superheated Belpaire boilers, equated to a virtually new engine! Still, sixty years or running must have realised a money back situation even with all the extra expense involving two rebuilds. No.40536 was another engine from the Carlisle (12) motive power area and was actually allocated to Upperby shed, but storage at 12A during 1955 would have been difficult because of the rebuilding of the engine shed and the remodelling of the shed yard. Prior to its time at Carlisle, where it had transferred in July 1954, the 2P had spent a couple of years at Buxton shed having arrived there from Spital Bridge shed. No.40536 had ended the LMS period at Leicester and moved to Peterborough in January 1952. *BLP - KRP 97F.3.*

The Barrow line-up from the west end of the shed yard in August 1955. Behind the two Furness 0-6-0s are 2P No.40396, also from Upperby. No.40536, and another, albeit unidentified, ex Midland 2P. On the left can be seen the rear wall of Barrow engine shed with its LMS period rebuilt roof, the shed itself dated from 1874 and had ten stabling roads, two of which ran through the shed at its northern end.. To the right is the manual coaling shed which was all the depot aspired to, with mechanical aids sadly lacking. Barrow was treated, like much of the Cumbrian area railway system, as something of a backwater compared to the rest of the LMS and later BR (LMR). A typical example of its standing during the modernisation period on BR was the allocation of the entire class of Metrovick Co-Bo diesel locomotives to cover the passenger and freight services. How to win friends amongst the public and inspire confidence and loyalty amongst your workforce - BR had some funny ideas during the transition period from steam to diesel. *BLP - KRP 97F.6.*

Date: April 1959. Location: Winsford, Cheshire. Whilst the new scrapping shop was being created at Crewe works, the rate of breaking up condemned locomotives slowed considerably so that it became necessary to store withdrawn engines wherever there was space available. One such place was the Over & Wharton branch on the Down side of the West Coast main line, some eight miles north of Crewe. Here, in the midst of the Cheshire countryside was created a dump where more than thirty locomotives were 'stored' for much of 1959. Amongst the various tank and tender engines was a bunch of former LMS (London, Tilbury & Southend section) tank engines which had been withdrawn during the previous February and brought north to Crewe for immediate despatch. However, they all ended up on the branch waiting for the final call. Centre stage here is 3P No.41945, latterly of Plaistow shed but known to have been resident at Tilbury during the early part of the decade. The 4-4-2T was one of the LMS Derby built examples of an earlier Whitelegg LTSR design, and had entered traffic in June 1927. It is hemmed in by two, Nos.41991 and 41992, of the goods '3F' 0-6-2Ts also from the drawing board of T.Whitelegg, and which entered traffic in November 1912, being built by Beyer, Peacock & Co., Manchester. These two had also arrived ex Plaistow shed. Other LTS line engines stored on the branch were: 41928, 41939, 41941, 41946, 41948, 41950, 41977, 41978, 41982, 41983, 41984, 41985, 41986, 41987, 41990 and 41993. The three engines featured here never did enter Crewe works and were sold instead to private yards; No.41945 went to Cashmores at Great Bridge whilst the two 3Fs undertook the long journey to Lanarkshire where Motherwell Machinery & Scrap Co. reduced them to small furnace size pieces. *BLP - DHB 1399.*

This elevated aspect reveals lots of detail for the modeller. Excepting the missing numberplate from the smokebox, No.41982 is still very much intact. Note the wrong facing British Railways crest on the tank side. Remember it was 'left is right and right is wrong'. Are wrong facing BR crests available in transfer/decal form for modellers? *BLP - DHB 1398.*

Just to the north of 0-6-2T No.41991, stood this superb example of London & North Western freight super power albeit redundant but nevertheless still impressive. Class G2A 7F No.49113 was one of fourteen withdrawn former LNWR 0-8-0 tender engines on the Over & Wharton branch in 1959, and had been condemned in January after working in south Wales since Nationalisation, latterly from Pontypool Road shed but entering British Railways at the LNW outpost at Abergavenny. Like most of the LNW 0-8-0s, No.49113 did not stay at one depot for too long and prior to its stint in Wales it had seen war service at Stafford, and before that Sutton Oak. note the tender cab which had been fitted at an unknown date but which was probably coupled when it transferred to Abergavenny. This 0-8-0 also made its final journey to Great Bridge. This line was closed to passenger traffic in June 1947, the LNWR terminal station at the end of the short branch was called Over & Wharton because there was another former LNWR station on the main line called Winsford which served the town also. The Cheshire Lines Committee had a station on the west side of the town and that was called Winsford too but it closed as early as January 1931. The disuse of the branch is evident from the foliage trying to overgrow the tracks, and over the dozen years following the demise of the passenger service not much else traversed the branch other than redundant rolling stock and now, redundant locomotives. The derelict line leading off to the top of the picture went to one of the numerous salt works which at one time dotted the landscape between the WCML and the River Weaver in this area. *BLP - DHB 1400.*

Although published before, this view of the Winsford line-up in 1959 deserves a place in this album if only to convey the impressive sight of so many former LNW 0-8-0s all facing the same way. There are nine of them in this view, and another five beyond the bridge in the distance. Some tender detail reveals that two of those present, including the one with a cab (49180), have footsteps on the rear sheet whilst the others are bereft of such. The footsteps would have been an LMS if not BR addition. The LNW would not waste money and materials on such niceties; after all, why fit footsteps when the fireman can access the water filler by way of climbing over the coal! Note also that all of the tanks engine bar one (No.41928), are also facing the same way. Just level with the tender of No.49308 is a gradient post which shows the line becoming level towards the cameraman whereas the engines are all stabled on the 1 in 100. *N.E.Stead.*

Ex 'Lanky' 3F No.52549 bathes in the evening sun at Bacup engine shed on 19th September 1954, just days away from withdrawal. The 0-6-0 was about to make a one-way journey to Horwich works for two reasons, its boiler was due for renewal and its home depot, Bacup shed, was about to close, with its small allocation being dispersed to other depots. No.52549 was obviously deemed to be surplus to requirements but it was pushing forty-two years of age and that cab was not what footplatemen wanted anymore (though they did not normally have a choice). Without taking into account the mechanical necessity of scrapping the engine, the reasons for its demise could virtually fill a sheet of paper - loss of traffic, changes traffic patterns, BR Standard classes, etc. - it was 1954! Being something of a youngster in comparison, the 2-6-4T in the background, No.42650, was sent to Bury on the closure of Bacup shed. After the Christmas period traffic was over and done with it moved on during the following January and was sent to Yorkshire to work from the likes of Low Moor, Copley Hill and Wakefield depots. By the time that British Railways came into being Bacup shed rarely housed more than a dozen locomotives which consisted a evenly balanced mixture of pre and post Grouping types. The aforementioned Stanier Class 4 tank, was about as modern as the fleet got before the 1954 closure and Bacup maintained four of them to cover the passenger services to Manchester. *BLP - KRP 23H.8.1.*

Situated in the industrial area of Sheffield known as Brightside was an engine shed known and indeed listed as Grimesthorpe. The latter name was perhaps a more appropriate title for the district but without insulting the people of Sheffield any further we will look at the subject to hand. This is former Midland Johnson 2F 0-6-0 No.58276 in open storage outside the engine shed (the triple pitched roof of which can be seen in the background) at Grimesthorpe on Sunday 17th October 1954. The old-timer was about to spend the winter in this yard, braving the elements until its services were required during the following year's traffic demands. Already fifty-seven years old, the 2F is looking dilapidated and unkempt, the gloom of the day reflecting its future. The storage of the 0-6-0 was typical of the steam age requirements whereby seasonal traffic patterns dictated the number of locomotives needed for the job; at any one time during the winter months up to 15% of the steam locomotive fleet would be in some kind of storage. No.58276 never did properly recover from this period of storage and although not withdrawn until June 1956, it is depicted here as waiting for the inevitable call to Derby works and breaking up. *BLP - KRP 26H.8.5.*

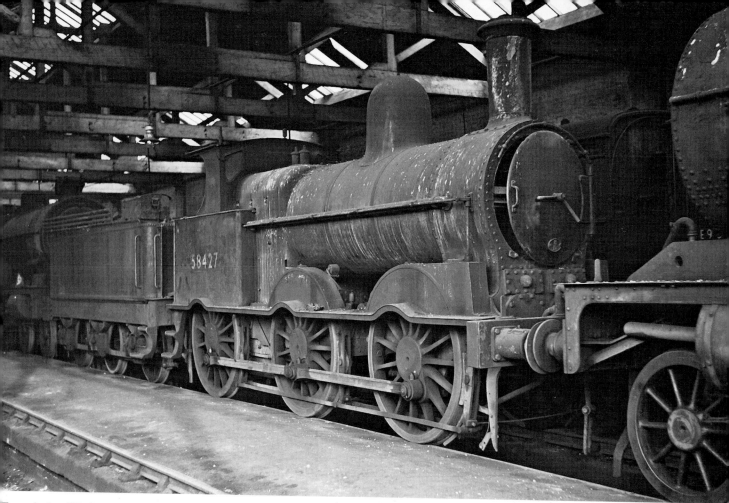

Even during BR days the former divisions at Trafford Park engine shed were kept well and truly alive with stored former LMS engines being housed in the one time LMS (Midland) section of the shed whilst ex LNER engines kept to their portion of the building. This is former LNWR 'Cauliflower' No.58427 stuck in between two stored Compounds on Sunday 14th August 1955. Although allocated to Widnes 8D shed in December 1954, the 0-6-0 has ended up in store at Manchester rather than at one of the depots in the Edge Hill motive power district. No doubt the spare stabling capacity at this former Cheshire Lines shed on the western edge of the city has attracted the Crewe-built goods engine. Other engine sheds attracted the old, clapped out and unwanted motive power and Widnes certainly attracted a fair number of this class during BR days with no less than a dozen (nearly half of the BR survivors) of the former LNWR 0-6-0 tender engines gracing its six roads up to their final demise at the end of 1955. Prior to its transfer to Widnes, No.58427 had spent a year at Stoke and before that four years at Edgeley shed in Stockport. Note that the engine has no chimney covering but it is under cover so atmospheric damage would be minimal. The same cannot be said for the paintwork though and the pigeon droppings give the 2F the appearance of a monument. Having been at Trafford Park since the previous April, the waiting is nearly over for No.58427 and come December the call to Crewe will see a swift end. *BLP - KRP 93F.1.*

Plodder Lane engine shed in Bolton was one of those establishments which got on with the daily drudge of supplying locomotives for the general movement of trains around the south-eastern area of the Lancashire coalfield. Its charges were mainly 0-8-0 tender locomotives of London & North Western origin and LMS built 4F 0-6-0 tender engines with a distinctive Midland pedigree. To look after a scant passenger service from Bolton's Great Moor Street station, the depot had a handful of useful tank engines, again of LNWR origin but which latterly, and up to closure, had been replaced by half a dozen motor-fitted LMS Ivatt 2-6-2 Cl.2 tank engines. This is a view of the depot on Sunday 10th January 1954 with what could be described as 'the usual crowd' at home for the weekend. The six road northlight roof shed was the last vestige of a larger complex which also comprised another northlight shed but of just four stabling roads which stood on the left of the picture - the white-washed rear wall stands as evidence of its location. The four-road shed, which dated from 1875 was demolished about 1950, after being disused since 1944, whilst this building dated from 1891 and was, as can be seen, in dire need of a replacement roof. However, the new roof was never to materialise as this place was planned for closure as BR struggled to make certain parts of its Lancashire railway system pay. Closure took place on Sunday 10th October 1954 and the allocation at that time was dispersed as follows: 0-8-0s Nos.49034, 49147, 49149 (nearest the camera) to Patricroft, No.49315 to Springs Branch; 0-6-0s Nos.44237, 44261, 44356 to Warrington Dallam, No.44384 to Heaton Mersey then Dallam, No.44473 to Willesden. The Ivatt 2-6-2Ts had dispersed gradually during 1954 with No.41210 leaving in March for Dallam whilst No.41214 went at the same time to Rugby. No.41213 was there at the end went to Walsall. Lone 'Jinty' No.47401 went with the big engines, down the road to Patricroft. The severity of the closure started to make itself felt in 1953 when No.44454 had transferred to Workington in the summer, followed by Nos.41212 and 41215 with 41216 which went to Bangor and Chester Northgate sheds respectively. So, there we have a case of not one withdrawal taking place but instead we have a shed closure and demolition shortly afterwards. *BLP - KRP 142.*

Now we have a double dose of 'waiting' with two Aspinall Lancashire & Yorkshire products, '27' or 'A' class 0-6-0 No.52349 and '23' class 0-6-0 saddletank No.51519. The venue is Horwich works on Sunday 19th September 1954 and both locomotives have just failed inspections which decided their futures - scrap. The 0-6-0ST appears to have failed a boiler inspection and the dome cover has been left on the front section of the tank giving the engine a new profile, albeit temporary. No.51519 has come the short distance from Bolton, its home shed for the last ten years of its life but now its end is imminent and come Monday morning it will be dragged to the east end of the works site and dismantled. The same fate awaits the A class too but its reason for withdrawal seems less apparent and its relatively clean turn-out suggests some kind of catastrophic failure after a recent visit to works for a new smokebox. The Sutton Oak based 0-6-0 was not one of the well travelled members of the class and spent all of its life in Lancashire. Of note are the LMS markings on both engines, more than six years after the demise of that company - not quite a record perhaps but worthy of note for modellers and historians. *BLP - KRP 22H.8.2.*

The dead engine line at Burnden shed, Bolton, in October 1958 with Lanky 'A' class No.52443, from Bury shed, heading a row containing four other engines. Next along is Fowler 7F No.49592 from Newton Heath with 'Jinty' No.47440, also ex 26A, sandwiched against another 7F 0-8-0, No.49662, a resident of Burnden shed. Finally, Fowler 4F 0-6-0 No.44000 of Skipton, brings up the rear. All these engines were waiting to visit Horwich works and being the nearest depot to the workshops, Bolton shed was used as the reception for most of the works intake. Similarly those engines which had undergone overhauls or repairs at Horwich were brought to Bolton shed for any running-in requirements. Besides emptying tender bunkers of any coal - when staff were available - Bolton would marshall the engines into groups for towing the short distance to Horwich. However, this lot were destined never to visit that workshop, or any other for that matter, ever again although the 'A' class appears to need some remedial work to the front bufferbeam which, it will be noted, is missing a couple of important components. The two 7F 0-8-0s never worked again and were condemned the following spring whilst the 0-6-0T and 4F were not condemned until the following December. All five of this lot ended up in the hands of the Central Wagon Co. at Wigan and were eventually cut up there during 1961. Postscript: Some two years later - November 1960 - the above group were still in the same position at Burnden engine shed, by which time they had been joined by a few more engines. *BLP - DHB 2884.*

Another aspect of the doomed group at Bolton in October 1958, looking from the west. All of them look fairly derelict with windows and other parts missing and it would be safe to say that none of them had worked for some time. *BLP - DHB 2888.*

Fowler Class 3 No.40063 was withdrawn in August 1962 but the Newton Heath based 2-6-2T had actually been laid up at Bolton shed sinc early 1958 in the company of other members of its class also from Newton Heath - Nos.40013, 40014, 40062 and 40065 - stored in a apparently serviceable condition. This is the tank on 14th April 1958 looking as though it is merely laid up for the weekend, although it i standing on the tracks reserved for the Horwich works 'intake'. Of it companions, No.40013 was condemned in December 1959 and take to Derby a few months later. No.40014 was the next to go in May 1960, destination Derby. However, both these Fowler tanks were the hauled from Derby to Doncaster, in March and June respectively, where spare capacity brought dozens of former LMS engines for cuttin up at the Plant scrapyard. In the meantime, the first of the five engines to be withdrawn, No.40065 in November 1959, went to Gorto works in May 1961 for breaking up. No.40062's departure was more rapid and after being condemned in November 1960 it was insid Crewe works cutting up shop within weeks. No.40063 was the last to leave this place when it finally reached Horwich works in Septembe 1962, a month after being condemned. Nos.40062, 40063 and 40065 were all seen at Bolton in November 1960, languishing inside th engine shed, away from the elements - goodness knows why but it was a 'funny' period on British Railways at the time. *BLP - KRP 217.2.*

Having finally made it to Doncaster 'Plant' works, there was no turning back for Fowler 2-6-2T No.40013. It is Sunday 20th March 1960 and the Class 3 tank, still wearing number and shed plates note, is spending its last weekend as a locomotive prior to being cut up at some time during the next six days. The somewhat circuitous route which took No.40013 from its original place of storage to its venue of demise is worth a closer look as to how BR was working at different levels, with different ideas, some twelve years after formation. The nearest works to Bolton shed was Horwich but because the engine had originally been the responsibility of Derby it was sent there. On the way it passed Gorton works and to some extent Crewe was actually nearer to Bolton than Derby. However, Derby must be obeyed even though at that time the place was bulging with stored, withdrawn and condemned locomotives of all shapes and sizes. Eventually, in a fit or common sense, or was it panic, somebody decided to send some of these silent hulks to Doncaster works for scrapping. Now, correct me if I am wrong but BR was once or twice reprimanded, by all and sundry, for wasting money, a charge which they strongly denied. *George Devine.*

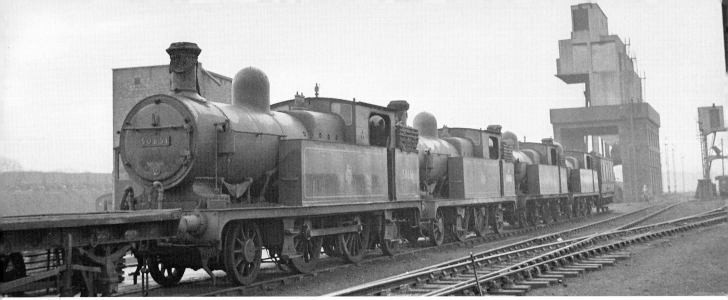

Rose Grove is best remembered for its allocation of Stanier Cl.5s and 8Fs in the final years prior to the end of steam on BR but during an earlier age, 1954 to be exact, the depot had more of a Horwich 'feel' than the later Crewe domination. Although many of the heavy freight locomotives resident at Rose Grove at that time were of the WD 'Austerity' kind, the 0-6-0 tender engines and many of its passenger tank were ex L&YR and were getting a bit 'long in the tooth' so to speak. This line-up on 10th January 1954 (top) contains four of the depot's Aspinall 2-4-2Ts (50651, 50652, 50653 and 50655) laid-up for the winter. The lower illustration dates from 19th September when just two remained, Nos.50655 and 50651. The other two were actually back at work but for these two time was running out. No.50651 was condemned in December whilst No.50655 managed to last out until June of the following year after a short sojourn to Bolton. BLP - KRP 137 & 22H.8.8

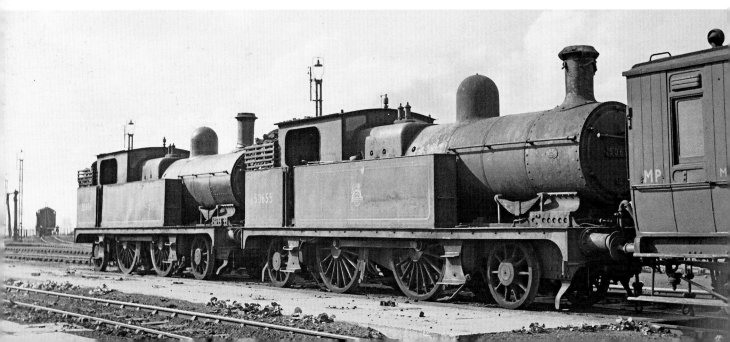

The Slag Reduction Co. site at Holmes in Rotherham and some of its more celebrated temporary residents have already been illustrated and mentioned in this album so with the introductions out of the way we review the other end of the yard on 17th October 1964 with ex LMS 4MT 2-6-4T No.42446 standing amongst some of the tenders belonging to the WD 2-8-0s on the site. Ex LMS 4F No.44531 is also in the frame but for that engine the waiting is over as the scrapmen have already cut into its firebox. The permanent way (perhaps best described as 'temporary way' but it appears to be better than a lot we have seen on BR property so far) had been specially laid to bring these locomotives onto the premises. How many locomotives the Company had in mind to purchase for scrap is unknown but the effort and cost of bringing this lot, not to mention the haulage by BR cost, must have been substantial. Rumours at the time (railway enthusiasts enjoy their quota of rumours from time to time) indicated that the purchasers were not too happy about the copper content of the engines and apparently expected more than what they actually got. On this date the residents included, besides those already mentioned, Nos.43880, 43903, 44172, 44286, 44304, 44327, 44333, 44531, 44543, 90197, 90324, 90371, 90403, 90525, 90548, 90564, 90618, 90646, 90708, 90715. Most of them had the fireboxes taken out. The number of locomotives being dealt with at this place, whilst it was operational, is somewhat sketchy but by 1965 the operation was wound up, even though there was plenty more scrap to be had from BR. *Malcolm Castledine.*

Although heavily vandalised, these two Ivatt Cl.2 tanks, Nos.41220 and 41233, are still very much intact at Edgeley shed in March 1967. Ironically these high mileage 2-6-2Ts arrived at 9B from Llandudno Junction shed in August 1965 to replace four low mileage BR Standard Cl.2 2-6-2Ts Nos.84013, 84014, 84017 and 84026. The latter engines had been chosen by BR to be despatched to Fratton shed and made ready, with slight modifications, for further work on the Isle of Wight. It looked as though the Standard tanks had 'got it made' and were about to work out their final days (years more like) overseas on a job which would have been hardly taxing. However, as they were assembled at various LMR sheds, along with six others of their kind, cancellation of the I-o-W scheme was announced in November 1965 and the ten Cl.2 tanks were all sent back from whence they came. No.84014 actually undertook the journey south and got as far as Basingstoke before a hotbox thwarted its progress over the remaining couple of dozen miles. After repair at Eastleigh it returned to the north. Edgeley withdrew all four on their return because although they were mechanically sound, there was no suitable work for their kind. They were sold for scrap and sent away for cutting up in March 1966 - the last of the BR Standard Cl.2 tanks. One of them was only eight years old! Back to our duo here, which had come to Stockport to work the pilot turns at Stockport (Edgeley) station vacated by the 'Isle of Wight Four'. No.41220 was of course motor-fitted with a vacuum control regulator (VCR) but that equipment was hardly required at 9B. The pair plodded on for a year, doing very little in reality because the 350 h.p. 0-6-0 diesel shunters had taken over what yard work still existed. Withdrawal took place on Saturday 12th November 1966. The waiting had started but would end six months later in May 1967 when the Ivatt tanks went together to Great Bridge and the scrapyard of the late John Cashmore. *BLP - DHB 8455.*

Edgeley engine shed was subordinate to Longsight in Manchester and although most of the important north-south expresses called at Stockport to pick up and set down passengers, engine changing of the expresses was not a requirement hence 9B had an allocation which reflected its secondary role with secondary traffic. Goods trains were the diet of the shed so goods engines and mixed traffic locomotives became the norm. No fancy 'namers' here, not even one calling in whilst passing. 9A had all the glamour whilst 9B took care of the mundane. One day however, things changed drastically, Edgeley was given a couple of new jobs to perform - overnight mail trains which passed through Stockport en route between their originating points in Yorkshire, west Wales and the south Midlands. At first Stanier Class 5s were transferred in then 9B got some 'namers', nothing fancy at first just a couple of 'Jubilees' in the shape of Nos.45596 BAHAMAS, and 45632 TONGA, in July 1962. Then, in September came No.45678 (I wonder who has that number plate) DE ROBECK but it was condemned in December having suffered a broken frame, so No.45732 SANSPAREIL replaced it in January but it was condemned in March 1964, only to be replaced by No.45654 HOOD. No.45670 HOWARD OF EFFINGHAM was transferred in September 1964 but was withdrawn a couple of weeks later. In August and October 1965, Nos.45632 and 45654, respectively, left for Newton Heath leaving behind what was probably Edgeley's most renowned locomotive - No.45596 which worked from 9B until withdrawn in September 1966. In the meantime, the big boys started arriving in the shape of three 'Britannia' Pacifics: Nos.70004 WILLIAM SHAKESPEARE, 70015 APOLLO and 70026 POLAR STAR in June 1965, followed by two more, Nos.70021 MORNING STAR and 70044 EARL HAIG, in May 1966. No.70044 was condemned on 24th October 1966 and left Edgeley for a scrapyard in Beighton in the following February. No.70026 was condemned 14th January 1967 and was sold to Cashmore's yard in Newport, departing in mid-April. Nos.70004, 70015 and 70021 carried on at 9B until transferred to Carlisle in June 1967 and that was the end of the 'namers' at 9B, a brief but nevertheless colourful episode in the history of the depot and appropriately at the end. This is No.70026 at Edgeley in March 1967 with just a few weeks to go before haulage to South Wales and oblivion. From this angle an appreciation of the massive firebox can be gained. *BLP - DHB 8453.*

Although it spent much of the summer of 1959 stored in a serviceable condition outside Royston shed, former Midland Deeley 3F 0-6-0 No.43789 was brought out of its slumber and revived to continue working into 1962. The vagaries of coal production in the Yorkshire field could see the likes of Royston's 3F population thrown into redundancy at the drop of a hat but seasonal ebbs and flows also played a part in the working life of a steam locomotive. Although the line-up here includes a 2P 4-4-0, the rest of the engines are 0-6-0 tender engines waiting for the winter demands to require their muscle. *George Devine.*

Ex Midland 3Fs, Nos.43680 (above) and 43687 languish at Saltley shed on 24th February 1963 some seven months after being condemned. Both are ready for the one-way journey to Cashmores at nearby Great Bridge. *Both Malcolm Castledine.*

The redundant sidings at Chaddesden, and at Spondon Junction, just to the east of Derby works, each became something approaching a mini Barry during the late Fifties'. When the sidings were initially used for engine storage, they contained mainly locomotives with Midland parentage but as the years marched on, engines from the Stanier stable started to collect there too. However, that event was to be some time off when newly arrived condensing 'Jinty' No.47210 became a resident in June 1959. Ex Cricklewood shed, the 0-6-0T had made the journey up from London after a short period of storage at 14A. Due for overhaul, the near fifty-years old tank was immediately condemned and then put into the sidings at Spondon Junction to wait in the queue for a buyer. Within a year the buyer had turned up, money changed hands and No.47210 was towed away to Killamarsh and broken up. The space was filled with another condemned locomotive and the cycle continued until about late 1964. *BLP - DHB 2730.*

They did not even bother to bag the chimney. 'Princess Royal' No.46200 at Upperby shed, July 1964. It is, by now, somewhat late for this graceful Pacific to follow the rest of the condemned members of the class into oblivion at Crewe works. Instead, this fallen lady will have to be taken to a private yard in Scotland where the inevitable would take place. It is coming up to two years since No.46200 was withdrawn but its external appearance is still reasonable. *BLP - DHB 6861.*

Just to prove that we are not totally biased towards steam locomotives in this album, we include this view of a group of former LMS carriages waiting to enters Drapers scrapyard at Hull on 8th October 1967. They were photographed in the sidings adjacent to Dairycoates engine shed in Hull and known locally as No.7 Section. For those of you interested in carriages they were numbered M27199M, M26656M, M26232M, and E13088M. *Mike Lake.*

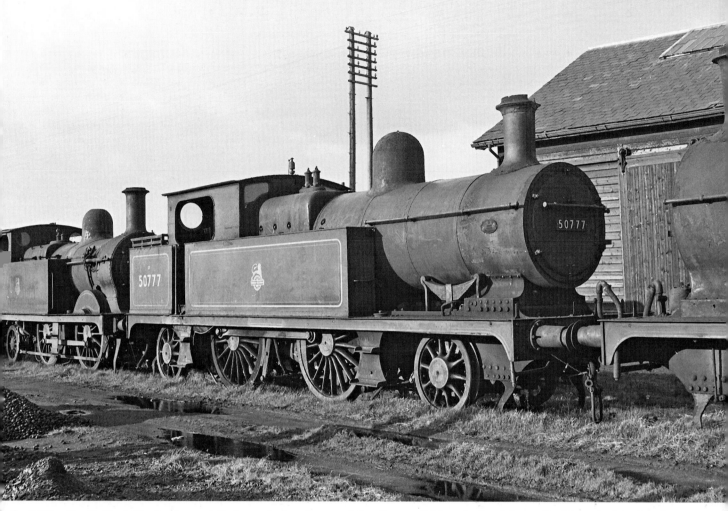

Badnall Wharf in Staffordshire has been visited once before in one of the albums of this series but it is worth taking a look at the place, and some of its occupants once again, to refresh our memories of what that particular dump was all about. Created in 1959, the dump was situated in sidings on either side of the West Coast main line some two miles north of Norton Bridge station. In common with the Winsford dump, the engines residing here were originally destined for the scrap shop at Crewe works but because of the modernisation of the Crewe facilities, the would-be customers had to wait their turn before being dealt with. As things turned out, the new facility at Crewe took longer to create than planned and meanwhile the 'customers' were becoming too many to handle so it was decided to put the Badnall lot up for tender just like the Winsford crowd. Most of the engines at Badnall Wharf consisted former Lancashire & Yorkshire tank engines with a mixture of ex Midland locomotives too, all old-timers. Here, in May 1959, we see Class 2P 2-4-2T No.50777 with exMR 4-4T No.58066 behind. This is the Up side site with just four engines in occupancy and in this view, No.51453 steals into the picture on the left whilst No.50855 shows part of its running plate and buffers. The Down side sidings had sixteen occupants at this time and more were to come. When Crewe did start scrapping with a vengeance in August, the imput from other parts of the Region was such that the Badnall lot never got a look-in and private contractors were invited to look once more. However, by then No.50777, along with two other exL&Y 2-4-2Ts had gone to Albert Looms yard in Spondon and were cut up before Crewe lit its first cutting torch. *BLP - KRP 211.7.* 37

EASTERN & NORTH EASTERN REGIONS

W. RIGLEY WAGON WORKS - SCRAP YARD, BULWELL FOREST, NOTTINGHAM: Primarily engaged in the building, repairing and scrapping of wagons, William Rigley's established a scrap yard here in Bulwell Forest, Nottingham in late 1963 alongside their existing works. Situated on the north side of the junction of the former Great Northern Leen Valley and Derbyshire Extension lines, from Basford to Colwick, via Mapperley tunnel, the yard was just west of Daybrook station. When the company purchased its first condemned steam locomotives for breaking up, the line through Mapperley tunnel was closed and so all traffic had been diverted via Nottingham Victoria station. The lack of traffic on the closed route meant that stabling room for purchased withdrawn locomotives was available without interfering with BR traffic and so the scene was set for a brief but lucrative period of scrapping redundant steam locomotives. During the year long period when this yard was taking in the steam locomotives, some interesting engines appeared before vanishing forever. The breaking-up of the engines seemed to take second place to the scrapping of wagons and so it took nearly a year (virtually the whole of 1964) for the yard to deal with the thirty locomotives which arrived. Those locomotives known to have been cut up are as listed: LMS 'Crab' 42792; LMS Reb. 'Patriot' 45535; LNER B1 61126, 61334; LNER K1 62013, 62032, 62038; LNER O4 63914; LNER O2 63925, 63926, 63927, 63928, 63932, 63935, 63936, 63937, 63938, 63939, 63941, 63945, 63956, 63962, 63964, 63972, 63973, 63974, 63977, 63980, 63985, 63987.

opposite) **As can be gleaned from the list, the exLNER O2 class 2-8-0 seemed to be the staple diet for the yard and most of those came from either Grantham or Retford sheds. This quartet of O2s sit on a siding near Daybrook station, on Sunday 22nd March 1964, prior to being hauled into the nearby yard. In early January at least three other O2s and their tenders had been reduced to scrap. Later, however, the engines entered the yard minus their tenders and local observers suggest that the tenders were cut up on separate occasions and the company seemed to run a regime whereby wagon work came first, the next stage involved reduced wagon work and cutting up tenders, and finally when little or no wagon work was available the engines were hauled in for despatch.** *Malcolm Castledine.*

Later that year, on Saturday 12th September 1964, five more O2s and a Peppercorn K1, all tenderless, await their turn to be dragged down the line for cutting up. Besides K1 No.62013, the O2s in the line-up were Nos.63956, 63980, 63939, 63985 and one unidentified. *Malcolm Castledine.*

On the same sunny September day, just a few yards further to the west, another Peppercorn K1, No.62032 awaits the inevitable and appears that a section of the cab roof signals a prelude to breaking up. Next in line is Rebuilt 'Patriot' No.45535, formerly SIR HERBER WALKER K.C.B., which had been withdrawn at Carlisle Kingmoor nearly a year previously. This was the area of the Rigley's works wher the dismantling took place although tidy at this moment in time, the ground would soon be littered with metal. *Malcolm Castledine.*

A week later and th K1 has been wheeled i along with O2 No.6395 Nos.63980, 63939 an 63985 wait for thei turn. Notice the fro numberplate still attache to No.63939's smokebo - they were an honest lo those Nottingham lad *BLP coll..*

Once a locomotive was withdrawn from Running Stock, it was not automatically sent for scrap. Indeed a number of engines ended up, for short periods at least, on Stationary Boiler duties at engine sheds mainly but also at other locations such as carriage sheds, workshops, or, as happened to one D11/2, warming a railway owned hotel. On Saturday 6th June 1959, withdrawn D16/3 No.62588 was carrying out S.B. duties at Stratford Locomotive Works but that job, which the 4-4-0 had performed since the previous October, was about to end. Not quite fifty years old when it was finally condemned, the engine had been employed at Stratford as a temporary steam supplier and the boiler (No.23376) was apparently never designated a number in the Eastern Region S.B. inventory. During its time serving the Great Eastern, the LNER and BR, No.62588 had been allocated to eleven different engine sheds, two of which - Botanic Gardens in Hull and Trafford Park, Manchester - were far removed from its GER roots. Its last shed was Cambridge where it worked for its last four months of operational life prior to this final duty. It was cut up at Stratford shortly after this scene was captured. Leaning into the picture from the right, J39 No.64715 was also withdrawn. Having been condemned during the previous month, the thirty-three year old former Colwick allocated 0-6-0 was about to be broken up and it too would leave this place in small pieces. Of interest to the modeller perhaps is the position of the set of bufferstops sandwiched between the two locomotives. They were installed to stop the enthusiastic shunting of dead engines disturbing the 'fixed' 4-4-0 which, as can be seen, was fairly well attached to the steam pipe connected to its dome. Keep that fact in mind next time you create a Stationery Boiler situation on your layout. *George Devine.*

Amongst the first Eastern Region locomotives purchased by private scrapyards were these two Gresley K2s seen at Doncaster shed on a rather damp Sunday 6th December 1959. Both engines were destined for the Motherwell Machinery & Scrap Co. at Wishaw, Motherwell having been secured by that firm on 28th October last. Nos.61743 and 61750, both from Boston shed, had been condemned on 22nd June 1959 and were now awaiting haulage to Scotland and their eventual doom. Neither engine were strangers to Scotland because since the end of World War Two, along with all the other England based members of the class, they had attended Cowlairs works in Glasgow for all their major overhauls. This time however it was to be a one-way journey north of the border. Altogether nine of the K2 class were scrapped at MM&S. The last reported sighting of our pair was on Tuesday 15th December near Leeds, when the duo were making their way north via the Settle & Carlisle route behind Skipton based 4F 0-6-0 No.43893. *George Devine.*

The end of 1959 was basically the end of the Gresley B17 class too. Any visitor to Doncaster Plant works during this period would have noted a fair number of the class awaiting cutting up. Indeed a large number of condemned engines were waiting for the completion of the new and enlarged scrapping facilities, complete with overhead crane. This is B17 Part 1 No.61625 RABY CASTLE, which had been condemned on Thursday 3rd December (note the name, number, works and shed plates still affixed), and was in the queue for the scrapyard on Sunday 6th December 1959. Behind is Part 6 derivative No.61658 THE ESSEX REGIMENT (also condemned 3rd December), with A3 No.60104 SOLARIO (the first A3 to be withdrawn - condemned the day after this scene was captured on film) bringing up the rear. Other B17 class on the works for scrapping at this time were Nos.61647 HELMINGHAM HALL (condemned 18th November 1959), 61654 SUNDERLAND (condemned 6th November 1959), and 61662 MANCHESTER UNITED (condemned 1st December 1959, and actually standing on the road behind this lot but not cut up until Monday 15th February 1960). *George Devine.*

Throughout 1959 the B17 class took a hammering - literally. This is Part 6 engine No.61665 LEICESTER CITY seen at Doncaster on Sunday 5th July waiting to be reduced to scrap. For all intents and purposes, and also because of its completeness, the photograph could have been depicting the engine at Stratford shed, for instance, awaiting its next duty. Withdrawn on Thursday 16th April, on arrival at the Plant works, the former Yarmouth based 4-6-0 is fairly clean and is carrying the Great Eastern line target type headcode discs which some wag has apparently arranged into the Royal Train code although one disc is hidden. From new in January 1937 the engine was always coupled to a Group Standard tender as here. Interestingly, one of the short wheelbase tenders originally attached to the first forty-eight members of the class, stands behind the GS tender. It too is fairly clean whilst its former owner was probably already cut up. Because of its proximity to many of the country's iron and steel making plants, and indeed other heavy industry, Doncaster works sold off a lot of redundant though serviceable locomotive tenders which were ideal not only as liquid carriers but were also useful, after conversion, for transporting hot and heavy billets between different departments within a steel works complex. Perhaps the ultimate irony would find a former locomotive tender chassis being used to carry steel billets made from the scrap metal of the locomotive to which it was once attached! *George Devine.*

O4 No.63593 decorates the yard at the south end of Doncaster engine shed on 10th October 1965. Although the tender is topped up with coal, the engine appears to be less than ready for work and that was in fact the case because it had been condemned exactly one week previously. Besides the missing pipework, the unnatural lean of the front plate, buffer beam and buffers leads us to the conclusion that the 2-8-0 has had something of a heavy shunt. The impact seemingly brought off the cylinder cover too. The front spectacle glass has disappeared, either purloined to keep another O4 in traffic or because it was shattered in the incident - who knows. In days recently passed, the damage would have been easily repaired at main works under heading of a Casual Light repair. But it is late 1965 and although Cowlairs was handing out such repairs to other classes, this near fifty-three year old veteran must have been deemed as 'not worth the effort' or some such conclusion. So, this one-time Great Central locomotive went out in the end with a bang - of sorts - and within a month it was headed to the Beighton scrap yard of T.W.Ward for dismantling. Did anybody empty that tender or did the scrapmen keep warm during the winter courtesy of BR. Now, what is attached to the piece of rope tied to the handrail but with the other end disappearing inside the smokebox? Answers to the Publisher please but no prizes will be given as we only want to know. *Malcolm Castledine.*

Six Gresley N2s stand in the yard at Grantham shed to await the next stage of their journey to Doncaster 'Plant' in late September 1962. All six are ex King's Cross 'Top Shed' and still carried their 34A shedplates but were actually allocated to New England, at least on paper they were. Most of this lot were transferred from London to Peterborough at the end of May 1962, it is debatable if any of them actually did any work from New England shed before they were withdrawn on 16th September 1962. Besides No.69538, the other 0-6-2Ts apparently consisted 69535, 69568, 69575, 69583 and 69593. The six tanks, and a lone unidentified O2, are stored on the two roads sitting in the middle of Grantham depot's coal stacking ground, just to the east of the 'New' engine shed - the main line is visible on the left of the picture along with the signal which controlled light engine movements from the shed to the main line. Much of the coal 'on the ground' at this time came from stored or condemned locomotives en route to either main works or to private scrap merchants. Many of these engines did not actually reach the Plant works until February or March 1963; No.69538's arrival being recorded as of Tuesday 19th February. *BLP - KRP 292.4.*

Withdrawn 3rd November 1958, Gresley D49/2 No.62754 THE BERKELEY, of Botanic Gardens shed in Hull, had only got as far as the train shed of North Road passenger station in Darlington by 4th July 1959. Keeping the 'Hunt' company in this rather salubrious storage facility were two withdrawn A8 tanks, No.69863 (furthest from camera) and No.69864. No.69863 had also arrived at Darlington on 3rd November 1958, ex Sunderland, and was condemned on the same day. Formerly Whitby based, No.69864 (note the difference in bunker types with 69863), had been condemned on 29th October 1958 but did not arrive at Darlington until 12th January 1959. How these three came to be stored together at this place for so long is a mystery because the constant movement of condemned locomotives into the scrapyard from either the engine shed at Bank Top or the nearby locomotive works would find stabling space to be at a premium. The scrap yard was, of course, just around the corner, behind the photographer - the waiting for this 4-4-0 and its companion Pacific tanks was virtually over. *George Devine.*

Even before the new scrapping facility was commissioned, Doncaster's capacity for scrapping locomotives had always been quite formidable. In July 1959 this line of Ex Great Northern 0-6-0s, LNER Class J6, all now minus their tenders, appears just like a production line, which it was in a sense, but in reverse. Breaking up has started with a vengeance at the far end of the line whilst the engines nearest are still fairly intact, though missing dome covers. The waiting is virtually over for No.64198 and within three or four days it will cease to exist. The others in this rather melancholy line are, from right: Nos.64261, 64266, 64176 and 64215. They had come from far and wide for this gathering, arriving at Doncaster in late March or early April from Colwick, Doncaster, Hitchin, Hornsey and New England but it was only now that they were dealt with. During the course of 1959, whilst scrapping was held back because of the improvements being carried out, Doncaster managed to cut-up thirty-four J6. Also, the following met the same fate through the year: 2 Thompson A2/2, 24 B17, 1 J17, 7 N1, 29 N2, the W1, 1 Y1 and 2 Y3. You should see the list of stuff they went through during 1960! Note the lack of niceties' regarding the engine/tender connections - just torched through - it was the only way to do it if figures were to be met. *BLP Collection.*

SOUTHERN REGION

When British Railways was born, the newly created Southern Region, which was basically the former Southern Railway with the latter word changed to Region, had various options open to it as venues for cutting up condemned locomotives. The usual and obvious names crop up, all of which were locomotive workshops: Ashford, Brighton, and Eastleigh. However, during the transition period from Railway to Region, a group of sidings at Horley were used dismantle withdrawn steam locomotives. Locomotives have been cut up at this site since pre-Grouping days (1884 being the earliest reference) when condemned London, Brighton & South Coast Railway locomotives were dismantled by private scrap merchants at the sidings. The choice of this location, situated approximately halfway between Brighton and London, arose because the scrap merchants apparently objected to paying carriage on their purchases to the railway so the LB&SCR compromised and hauled the withdrawn engines to Horley sidings, carriage free. The sidings used during the BR period are not the exact ones used prior to 1903 as that particular venue was swallowed up during the quadrupling of the main line between Horley and Earlswood. Nevertheless, it is worth looking at the list of engines cut up at Horley during the post-war period when scrap metal was somewhat abundant. Undertaken when it was, Horley was essentially the last large venture undertaken by the private scrap metal firms, and for the following decade everything would seem to be controlled with BR taking care of its condemned locomotives. When the 'great pull' of steam locomotives, which was instigated by British Railways from 1960 onwards, started to take effect, BR itself was unable to cope with the large volumes of scrap it was making available and private industry was once again invited to tender for the scrap. They willingly stepped into the breach but even so the supply often outstripped demand and so 'dumps' were created to clear the clutter from the sheds.

Horley Scrap List 1949 and 1950 (all locomotives ex Southern Region but the list is not exhaustive):

B4 4-4-0	2074
C2 0-6-0	2436
D1 0-4-2T	2274
D1/M 0-4-2T	2215, 2234
E1 0-6-0T	2097, 2112, 2127, 2162, 2690
G6 0-6-0T	240, 262, 275, 354
K10 1MT 4-4-0	137, 140, 142, 144, 145, 151, 341, 344, 345, 386
L11 1MT 4-4-0	167, 168, 410, 435,
O1 0-6-0	1123, 1377
R1 0-4-4T	1699
T 0-6-0T	500S
T1 0-4-4T	5
X6 4-4-0	657

Total 34

Hiding away from but near to Three Bridges shed on 28th July 1954 was this former South Eastern D class 4-4-0 No.31591 in apparentl[y] serviceable condition but open storage. It had arrived at 75E during the previous January from Redhill shed and was immediately pu[t] into store, still wearing the 75B shed plate. By the end of the year it was returned to Redhill, on paper at least, transferred back befor[e] withdrawal. But then it was transferred to Guildford in February 1955 to join sister No.31586 but it is doubtful if the 4-4-0 went anywher[e] from here other than Ashford works. The Southern Region would store a fair percentage of their 'available' motive power during certai[n] periods of the year, not least during the winter. Therefore, it is highly unlikely that this engine was moved twice during the winter month[s] from its reasonably isolated haven here. Withdrawn in June 1955 at Ashford, it was cut up there a few weeks later - forty-eight years afte[r] it had emerged from the erecting shop as a new 'Coppertop'. Note the pile of briquettes in the tender. *BLP - KRP 13H.8.8.*

R1 0-4-4T No.31698 sits at the back of Tonbridge shed on 27th July 1954 with suitable protection enclosing its chimney. The former South Eastern & Chatham Railway tank was stored awaiting suitable traffic conditions which would enable it to get back into traffic. However, the R1 never did manage to work again and after a long period in store it was condemned in October 1955 and cut up at Ashford, its birthplace. Some fifty-five years old at the end, No.31698 was the penultimate survivor of the once fifteen strong class designed by Kirtley and subsequently rebuilt by Wainwright. Thirteen of the class entered British Railways employment and of those, seven were fitted for push-pull work but this engine was not amongst them and ended its life as seen here. *BLP - KRP 12H.8.7.*

Ryde engine shed, Isle of Wight, 30th July 1954. Two O2s are laid up for the 53/64 winter season but the winter has come and gone, its the height of summer. So, why has this pair still got all the rudiments of winter storage attached? Nos.19 OSBOURNE and 23 TOTLAND were in fact to undergo a longer term in storage than what they had already undergone. The stark truth was that neither of these two properly recovered from this 'storage' and No.23, along with No.34 NEWPORT made history by becoming the first IoW O2s to be condemned by British Railways in September 1955. No.23 was not far behind and became the third casualty during the following December. Note the neat little chimney cover worn by No.19 - no sacks here! *BLP - KRP 16H.8.4.*

Having just arrived from Nine Elms shed, where it was condemned, No.82029 waits for the inevitable at Salisbury in July 1967. Note that the coupling and connecting rods, lying precariously atop the water tank, do not appear to be secured in any way whatsoever! Did they travel down from London in that position? The BR Cl.3 2-6-2T had started life working from Darlington shed in December 1954. Three years later it moved to West Hartlepool but by the end of September 1958 had settled in a Malton but traffic was declining and Malton shed closed in 1963. In a final effort to find work for the engine, and its sisters Nos.82026, 82027 and 82028, the North Eastern Region sent it to York in April 1963 but most of its time at 50A was spent in open storage with the other three. The Southern Region beckoned with the promise of work for steam locomotives whilst that Region was still gearing up for electrification in 1967. So, at the end of September 1963 the four Standard Cl. 3 tanks moved on to pastures anew at Guildford. During the following January all four then transferred to Bournemouth but not for too long and by the cessation of the summer timetable they went east to Nine Elms for the final period of Southern steam workings. Of the four former NE Region tanks which seemingly followed each other around, no matter where, only this one lasted into 1967, its three sisters having succumbed at varying times during 1966. All four went to different scrap yards and when it's time came in November 1967, No.82029 was taken to Birds Commercial Motors at Risca although it is not known if those coupling rods were finally secured before the final journey. Also at Salisbury on this date was sister No.82019, the other Nine Elms Cl.3 which worked to the end of SR steam; it too went to Bird's at Risca. *BLP - DHB 9164.*

Next in line from No.82029 was USA 0-6-0T No.30072 which had sister No.30064 for company. After being evicted from Southampton docks by the newly acquired diesel fleet, No.30072 was sent in February 1963 to Guildford where it acted out the role of shed pilot until that depot closed on 7th July 1967 - the end of SR steam. Chalked graffiti with references to 'the end etc.' has been rubbed off but not totally eradicated from the tank sides and cab sheet for some reason - perhaps officialdom did not like the remarks; they were (BR hierarchy that is) slightly sensitive during those latter years of BR steam workings. Anyway, these two engines did not travel any further west than Salisbury as both ended up being purchased for preservation and were taken back to Eastleigh prior to travelling to their new homes and life after steam. Perhaps, because of their afterlife, the two USA tanks do not qualify to be illustrated in this album but this particular illustration shows just how near the pair got to being on the edge of oblivion. Others of their ilk which had recently staged through Salisbury and were not so lucky included Nos.30073 in May, 30061 in June, 30067, 30069 and 30071 in July, all bound for Cashmores scrap yard at Newport. *BLP - DHB 9165.*

'West Country' No.34006, sans nameplates and lots of other bits, languishes on the dead-engine line at Salisbury shed in July 1967. Withdrawn during the previous March, at this very shed, the once proud, twenty-two years old Pacific is awaiting a buyer. The representative from Cashmores was already on his way to Wiltshire and BUDE would soon be hauled away to Newport, Monmouthshire following in the treads of countless other Southern locomotives which ended their days being unceremoniously 'tended to' by Welshmen with cutting torches. From this angle it is apparent just how long the smoke deflectors were on these unrebuilt Pacifics - virtually a third of the total body length. No.34006 is officially credited with having run over the magic one million miles mark in traffic, a feat matched by just two others of the class; if figures are accurate BUDE actually held the record at 1,099,338 miles. This engine of course, along with sisters Nos.34004 and 34005, took part in the 1948 Locomotive Exchanges and was coupled to ex LMS tender No.10329, complete with water scoop, for the period of its absence from the SR although the actual coupling took place at Brighton works where any necessary temporary changes could be carried out to pipework, etc. Whilst it was in the works it was also given an overhaul which kept it out of traffic for ten weeks! The other two 'WCs' were also coupled to ex LMS tenders, Nos.10411 and 10346 respectively. Although equipped with the former LMS tender, No.34006 did not work over any part of the LM Region during its trials and instead worked over the old Great Central route of the Eastern Region between Marylebone and Manchester (London Road). Later it went to the Western Region for further trials over the Bristol-Plymouth section. As a further aside to the scene depicted here, it seems inconceivable now but in those heady days of 1948 it was possible to see two different but consecutively numbered Southern Pacifics at two separate Manchester termini on the same day. Never before and never again would such an event take place - although if a railtour was run into Man Vic. terminal platforms whilst another railtour was run to Piccadilly on the same day..... *BLP - DHB 9168.*

'Battle of Britain' No.34056 CROYDON had a few things in common with No.34006; it was allocated to Salisbury shed until withdrawn in May 1967. It went to the same scrap yard in south Wales, at virtually the same time. It was one of Bullied's Light Pacifics. There however we can draw the line because No.34056 was one of the sixty rebuilds whereas 34006 remained virtually in original profile. Of course we could go on about the differences....Eastern Section working...only coupled to one tender throughout, No.3306...etc., etc. One other detail worth mentioning which both had in common - high mileage. Although CROYDON never did reach the magic million, it came very close to it at 957,081 miles and considering the age difference would no doubt have made it if not for that eighteen months difference. Most of the others came nowhere near. The external condition of No.34056 is commendable compared with the Nine Elms and Eastleigh based Pacifics but the scrap merchants were not bothered one way or the other - scrap metal is metal, clean or dirty. Some of the other 'dead' engines stored at Salisbury on this day in July 1967 were: 34018, 34021, 34024, 34025, 34037, 34040, 34044, 34060, 34071, 34077, 34087, 34089, 34090, 34098, 34102, 34104, 34108, 35007, 35008, 35013, 35023, and 35030 (this engine hauled the last steam working into Waterloo on Sunday 9th July), and that was just the Pacifics. Others included a single Ivatt Cl.2 No.41312, nine BR Standard Cl.5s, and twenty-four other assorted Standards. *BLP - DHB 9169.*

An elevated aspect of the gathering at Weymouth Radipole engine shed on 28th July 1967 with rebuilt 'WC' No.34004 YEOVIL prominent amongst the throng. Although the name and number plates have been removed, the engine is very much intact. Cashmores Newport yard was the recipient for this engine which went west three months after this image was captured. For the record, the dead engines - and that was all of them - resident at Weymouth on this July day were: 34004, 34036, 34052, 34093, 34095, 35003, 35014, 35026, 41224, 41230, 41295, 41320, 73003, 73016, 73018, 73020, 73092, 75068, 75076, 76008, 76009, 76026, 77014 (which had apparently hauled the last steam arrival into Weymouth, a van train from Bournemouth - 9th July 1967), 80011, and 80134. Four of them, two Ivatt tanks and two Standard ?s, left the depot next day making the one-way journey to South Wales. Besides No.77014's slight claim to fame, three other engines in this group had also worked on the final day - No.34052, 34095 and 73092. *BLP - DHB 9202.*

'Merchant Navy' No.35003 and another of the class, No.35014, sandwich a BR Standard Class 4 tank between them. All the clues as to thi depots origin are plainly visible with the overgirder and pitless turntable being a standard Great Western Railway outside appliance. Th coaling stage in the distance is quiet now, its lifetime employment ended but its GWR features are plain to see. The coaler dated from the yard improvements of 1930 whilst the 65ft turntable was an earlier, 1925, improvement. Alongside the 'MN' is BR Standard Class No.73003 appearing to be standing there open-mouthed in disbelief as to the swiftness of the sudden mass cull. *BLP - DHB 9193.*

Number plates, shed plates, connecting and coupling rods - not to mention the reason for existence - all gone. BR Class Cl.4 No.76008 waits in line with a couple of ex LMS Ivatt Cl.2 2-6-2 tanks, Nos.41295 and 41230, for company on Friday 28th July. The latter pair were amongst the quartet beginning their ultimate trip the following day. *BLP - DHB 9194.*

Weymouth shed, 28th July 1967. Cl.2 No.41295 managed to keep its lining to the end, No.41230 on the other hand had lost it some time

before. *BLP - DHB 9195.*

Now here is one virtually intact. Green liveried Cl.5 No.73092 has lining on the cabside but the tender appears bereft; perhaps an exchange had recently taken place. The first signs of rot have appeared on the side sheet of the BR1C tender but that would not worry anyone, anymore. *BLP - DHB 9198.*

Although only just discernible, the legend on the side tank of Cl.2 No.41320 says it all. It appears that both this engine and the Standard 5 were amongst the last working examples at Weymouth and nobody has yet bothered to remove the coupling and connecting rods. Perhaps the fitters had all been laid off. The depot closed to steam on the evening of Sunday 9th July 1967 and this visit by Don Beecroft took place a couple of weeks later. However, the shed yard and indeed the shed itself was used until October 1970 to service visiting diesel locomotives. *BLP - DHB 9199.*

D class 4-4-0 No.31501 temporarily (for about seven years apparently) posing as a 4-2-0 whilst on Stationery Boiler duties at Ramsga[te] carriage shed on Monday 26th July 1954. The 'D' had been engaged on this duty since withdrawal from Faversham shed in 1953 and worke[d] until at least 1958 when an alternative heating method was installed at the carriage shed. From then until the end of 1960 it lay in th[e] same position, thought derelict and looking all the worse for a wooden shelter built around the cab. Apparently No.31501 never did get i[ts] missing wheel set back and was cut up on site whilst work was proceeding to eradicate steam motive power from the area. Note the wood[en] bodied snow plough drawn up to the tender - that might have been useful in 2009. It would be interesting to know how coal was got into th[e] tender because even though the engine was stationery, it would still burn a substantial amount each day when in use. Detaching the tend[er] on a regular basis and running it over to the coaling plant seems the most obvious method of keeping the coal supply going, other than usi[ng] manual labour. As for the water supply, that too would probably be got from the tender, as normal, and the tender itself topped up on i[ts] regular (winter) visits to the coaler and, where was the water supply? Only one injector was used and the clack valve on the right side of th[e] boiler (out of sight unfortunately) was connected by way of an external, and temporary looking, pipe to a source beneath the cab. Note th[e] various chocks/sleepers, etc., used to keep the engine stationary. When this engine took over these duties in the summer of 1953, it was n[ot] fitted with the tall chimney worn by the previous S.B., O class 0-6-0 No.A98 which had been in use at Ramsgate since 1929. *BLP - KRP 8H.8.[..]*

This scene at Nine Elms shed in May 1967 looks rather apocalyptic with not a soul in view and locomotives just left where they expired. Even the lattice girders supporting the remains of the shed roof add something of a skeletal ambience to the scene. Although complete closure of Nine Elms engine shed was still a couple of months away, the place was certainly rundown by now and how the staff managed to keep their engines working amidst all this dereliction and squalor was nothing short of a miracle. Centre stage here is BR Class 4 No.80012 with its motion lay on the floor beneath. The 2-6-4T had been here since withdrawal on 19th March and was probably condemned for want of a simple part replacement. Shortly after this scene was captured on film it was hauled away to Salisbury shed for storing (dumping) whilst a buyer was sought for its sixty-nine tons of scrap. Like most of the Southern Region engines it went to south Wales and ended up in the Newport yard of J.Buttigieg, one of only four of the class purchased by that company. *BLP - DHB 8545.*

The temporary scrapyard set up at Holmes by Steel, Peech & Tozer (Slag Reduction Co.) in Rotherham during 1964 became the fina
destination for many locomotives including a few dozen WD 2-8-0 from the north-west accompanied by a similar number of 4F 0-6-0s an
2-6-4Ts. However, three Southern Region locomotives which ended up there became something of celebrities amongst the enthusiasts wh
witnessed their presence. This is 'Merchant Navy' No.35002 on 17th October 1964, albeit without name or numberplates but nevertheles
unmistakably a Rebuilt MN, with its cabside number still legible. In front of the Pacific, is the tender from U class No.31793, albeit out o
frame here, which miraculously still carried its smokebox numberplate (I wonder what happened to that?). In front of the 'U' was anothe
'Merchant Navy' No.35015. The two Pacifics were in fact the first of their class to be withdrawn, a deed which took place in February 196
at their home shed - Nine Elms. The 2-6-0, formerly of Guildford shed, was also ex Nine Elms having been condemned in May 1964. B
Christmas all three of the 'visitors from afar' had been reduced to scrap. *Malcolm Castledine.*

astleigh works 31st July 1954. '0458' class 0-4-0ST No.30458 IRONSIDE has just retired and is waiting for the inevitable. Not quite aking its 65th birthday, this Hawthorn Leslie built locomotive would have been 'snapped up' for preservation some ten years later but it as not to be and the little four-coupled tank, albeit without any rods in this view, got the chop less than two months later. Being a 'one-off' n British Railways certainly had its drawbacks and no matter how much tender loving care was received by the engine, if a major failure ccurred, there was usually no spare. Its place at Guildford shed, where it worked as the pilot, was soon filled by a B4 tank and so the end or No.30458 was 'cut and dried', certainly the former. *BLP - KRP17H.8.8.*

SCOTTISH REGION

After Nationalisation many of the former LMS locomotives based in Scotland, especially the 2P 4-4-0s, were sent to Inverurie for overhaul and it was inevitable that many of them would end up there for breaking up after being condemned. Such a fate has befallen Nos.40606, 40610 and 40590 which had recently arrived from the west coast sheds at Ardrossan and Ayr respectively. It is 16th May 1959 and the trio had just started to have their tenders emptied of coal (how many memos went between workshops and running sheds requesting the latter to empty tenders before sending locomotives off to main works?), note the spillage on the ground but there was a wagon alongside No.40590's tender. Though not the first of their class to be withdrawn, these three engines were in fact the first of their class to be scrapped at Inverurie but they were not the last ones as twenty-four more were dealt with up to June 1962. No.40610 had already spent most of the winter in store, its work taken by BR Standard tank engines but all of these 4-4-0s had managed to get thirty years service in before their demise so, as a financial return, the accountants would have been happy at least. *BLP DHB 1759.*

In July 1959 K2 No.61791 LOCH LAGGAN was laid aside at Fort William shed, though its chimney was yet to be covered for long term storage. A resident of this former North British outpost for nearly twenty years, the 2-6-0 transferred here from Glasgow in July 1940, a good time, some would say, to be away from any city in the United Kingdom but nevertheless a pleasant location in which to be based throughout the war. With the coming of the Peppercorn K1s after Nationalisation the Gresley engines shared the duties on the West Highland line, be they passenger or goods. Later came the Stanier Class 5s which were hugely popular with the footplatemen, but with the impending arrival of the 'all-conquering' diesels at the end of the decade the somewhat long-in-the-tooth K2s became certain candidates for withdrawal. This monochrome picture does not quite convey the rust covered condition of the boiler cladding (for a similar though full colour view see Keith Pirt's Steam Colour Portfolio Scottish Region Vol.1) but it signified the end for the K2 and the dreaded deed took place in March 1960. At the end of the following month No.61791 was en route to Cowlairs for the chop. However, the BR works was becoming overwhelmed with condemned locomotives requiring cutting up so this 2-6-0, along with J39 No.64948, was sold to J.N.Connel, a scrap merchant located in Coatbridge. By the middle of June 1960 both locomotives had ceased to exist. The tender attached to No.61791 was one of the group which did not get the new BR crest and went for scrap with the old emblem still proudly displayed. Note that the Group Standard tender on the right (coupled to K1/1 No.61997 MAC CAILIN MOR) has the wrong facing example of the new BR emblem. *BLP - KRP 234.1.*

Grangemouth, Fouldubs 'dump' 17th May 1959 with a couple of Eastfield based D11/2s, No.62676 is just off camera to the left, two D34 'Glens' Nos.62472 and 62474, also from Eastfield, with three ex Caley 2P 0-4-4Ts Nos.55204 (Grangemouth), 55214 (Motherwell) and push-pull fitted 55238 (Grangemouth) bringing up the rear. Most, but not all, had their chimneys 'sacked' for long term storage and none were as yet withdrawn. Besides these engines, dozens more were laid up at other dumps around Scotland at this time. The storage lines were about to get longer and more diverse but on this date the venues visited included: Bathgate (18), Dundee (11), Forfar (16), Hurlford (7), Kittybrewster (18), Polmadie (18), Polmont (16), even Kilmarnock works, a long time venue for cutting up condemned locomotives was now being used to store both serviceable and withdrawn engines. Numerous other sites, engine sheds in the main, had two or more engines 'laid up' in some type of storage. Some of the occupants here never worked again. *BLP - DHB 1854.*

A corner of the Bathgate 'dump' on 17th May 1959 with D30 No.62439 FATHER AMBROSE prominent not just being centre stage but also being sacked and sans smokebox door handles. It was never to work again and was condemned during September. Other stored engines about the shed on this date were 47162, K3 No.61879, 62422, 62428, 62432, 62495, 64486, 68097, 68102, 68118, 68339, 68463, 68478, 69162, 69169, 69172 and 69220. Others which had recently come and gone included 56253, 62683, 64528, 68324, 68348, 69147, 69148, 69160, 69175, 69200. *BLP - DHB 1870.*

The former Glasgow & South Western Railway locomotive works at Kilmarnock was found to be surplus to requirements when British Railways came into being. However, it did find a new role repairing cranes and other mobile plant but it became well known, or is that infamous, for taking on a more sinister occupation - breaking up withdrawn locomotives. For more than ten years up to the cessation of scrapping in July 1959, the works steadily dismantled more than a couple of hundred redundant Scottish Region steam locomotives. The establishment was not adverse to taking in engines from other regions too. The mixture of classes was indeed diverse with former Highland engines rubbing shoulders with those from the pre-Grouping companies of the Caledonian, North British, Midland besides those built by the LMS and LNER. On Sunday 20th July 1958, some twelve months before closure, the works had its hands full after the recent increase in withdrawals brought on by dieselisation. This is D30 'Scott' class No.62434 KETTLEDRUMMLE, formerly of Dundee, sandwiched between a couple of ex Caledonian 0-4-4 tanks, or which McIntosh 2P No.55141 is nearest the camera. *George Devine.*

The precise number of engines scrapped at Kilmarnock after Nationalisation is unknown - no doubt someone, somewhere, will have the original record or log of those which passed through the place but without that document an informed estimate will have to suffice. Of course it would be easy enough to state that all Scottish Region engines withdrawn prior to Easter 1959 were dealt with at Kilmarnock but that was not the case, for the most part at least. During the period that Kilmarnock was active scrapping engines, the three BR workshops in Scotland still carrying out locomotive overhauls - Cowlairs, Inverurie and St Rollox - did occasionally scrap engines, either at the point when dismantling for repair was taking place and decisions were reversed or, during so-called 'slack periods' to keep the workforce employed. The small former Highland Railway workshop at Inverness was known to have scrapped a few engines during early BR days so that must also be included in the equation. The types known to have been cut up at Kilmarnock and their known number were: exLMS Group - 4P 4-4-0 59; 0-4-0 Sentinel 1; 3F 0-6-0T 1; exCR 4-6-0 6; exHR 4-6-0 2; exCR 4-6-2T 1; exCR 4-4-0 11; exHR 4-4-0 2; exCR 0-6-0 37; exHR 0-6-0 2; exCR 0-6-0T 12; exCR 0-4-4T 19; exCR 0-4-0ST 1; exLNER Group - C15 2; D11/2 1; D30 5; D33 1; D34 1; G5 1; J35 2; J36 7; J72 1; J83 7; J88 9; K2 9; N2 3; N15 16; V4 2; Y9 5. With vegetation sprouting up virtually everywhere within its boundaries, Kilmarnock certainly had the look and feel of an unkempt graveyard. Standing away from the main building on that Sunday in July 1958 was Gresley K2/2 No.61774 LOCH GARRY which had been condemned during the previous April but had lain in this deplorable condition at Eastfield shed for some time. Other noted occupants lying around the works premises intact on this date were: 0-4-0ST No.56030, J83 No.68474 condemned at St Margarets shed on 18th April 1958 after its cylinder walls collapsed in Calton tunnel whilst engaged in shunting), K2 No.61775 LOCH TREIG, and N15 No.69167. *George Devine.*

Greenock Princes Pier engine shed 1st August 1955. Tucked away in the north-west corner of this former Glasgow & South Western locomotive depot, and offering little interference to the everyday running of the shed, was a group of four stabling sidings which, by 1955 and much earlier too, were used to store laid-up and withdrawn locomotives. On this first day of August 1955 a small number of ex Caledonian 4-4-0s (Nos.54440, 54468, 54506 noted) were resident on the sidings along with an ex LMS 2P 4-4-0. None of the engines mentioned were as yet condemned but there time would come. No.54479 had already been 'laid-up' for a couple of years or so when captured on film and although it apparently did not work again, it was not withdrawn until October 1959, some months after the engine shed itself had closed. Eventually, in February 1960 it was purchased by a private scrap yard in Scotland. For the record Nos.54441 and 54453 were active at the shed, and employed in carrying out the passenger train duties which brought these capable 4-4-0s to this place in 1939. Now! about that desirable, and much sought after, terraced property overlooking a pleasant meadow of wild flowers, just a short walk from the promenade offering excellent vistas across the broad expanses of the lower Clyde..... *BLP-KRP 89F.6.*